Inside My Body

How do my braces work?

Steve Parker

Raintree
Essex County Council

www.raintreepublishers.co.uk
Visit our website to find out
more information about
Raintree books.

To order:
☎ Phone 0845 6044371
▤ Fax +44 (0) 1865 312263
▧ Email myorders@raintreepublishers.co.uk

Customers from outside the UK please telephone +44 1865 312262

Raintree is an imprint of Capstone Global Library Limited,
a company incorporated in England and Wales having its
registered office at 7 Pilgrim Street, London, EC4V 6LB –
Registered company number: 6695582

Edited by Kate de Villiers and Laura Knowles
Designed by Steve Mead
Illustrations by KJA-artists.com
Picture research by Mica Brancic
Originated by Capstone Global Library Ltd
Printed and bound in China by CTPS

ISBN 978 1 406 22108 4 (hardback)
14 13 12 11 10
10 9 8 7 6 5 4 3 2 1

ISBN 978 1 406 22120 6 (paperback)
15 14 13 12 11
10 9 8 7 6 5 4 3 2 1

British Library Cataloguing in Publication Data
Parker, Steve
How do braces work?. -- (Inside my body)
612.3'11-dc22
A full catalogue record for this book is available from the
British Library.

Acknowledgements
We would like to thank the following for permission
to reproduce photographs: Alamy p. **13** (© Pixel
Shepherd); iStockphoto pp. **24** (© Jozsef Szasz-Fabian),
15 (© Kirk Strickland); Photolibrary pp. **6** (age fotostock/
Gustavo Andrade), **21** (Corbis), **4** (Design Pics Inc), **7**
(Design Pics Inc/Chris Knorr), **16** (Digital Light Source/
Richard Hutchings), **10** (Flirt Collection/Jim Cornfield), **5**
(Imagestate RM/Michael L Peck), **18** (Moodboard RF), **8**
(Radius Images), **17** (Somos Images/Bill Varie); Science
Photo Library p. **20** (Tirot); Shutterstock pp. **14** (Adrian
Hughes), **25** (Paul Prescott), **27** (© Monkey Business
Images), **19** (© Ragne Kabanova).

Photographic design details reproduced with permission
of Shutterstock pp. **7, 9, 13, 15, 16, 21, 22** (© Isaac
Marzioli), **7, 9, 13, 15, 16, 21, 22** (© Yurok).

Cover photograph of girl with braces reproduced
with permission of Getty Images/Brand X Pictures/
Andersen Ross.

We would like to thank David Wright for his invaluable
help in the preparation of this book.

Every effort has been made to contact copyright holders
of any material reproduced in this book. Any omissions
will be rectified in subsequent printings if notice is given
to the publisher.

All the Internet addresses (URLs) given in this book were
valid at the time of going to press. However, due to the
dynamic nature of the Internet, some addresses may
have changed, or sites may have changed or ceased to
exist since publication. While the author and publisher
regret any inconvenience this may cause readers, no
responsibility for any such changes can be accepted by
either the author or the publisher.

Contents

Words that appear in the text in bold, **like this**, are explained in the glossary on page 30.

Why do some people wear braces?

Do you wear braces on your teeth, or do you know someone who does? Some children wear braces to help their teeth grow straight, without gaps or crowding that could cause problems when they grow up. A few adults wear braces too.

Why are teeth important?

There are many reasons why teeth are so important:

- You use them to bite and chew food before swallowing. This stops you choking on big lumps of food.
- Chewing also helps your body to digest the food well and get the most **nutrients** from it.
- You need teeth to speak properly. Try saying "the" without your tongue touching your teeth.

🔍 **If you are lucky, you will be able to choose what colour your braces are.**

Lots of teeth

An adult person has 32 teeth. This may seem a lot, but some animals have many more teeth. For example, some dolphins have as many as 250 teeth.

A tiger has 30 teeth. They include four very long, pointed ones, called canines.

What do my teeth look like?

How much do you know about your teeth? Keeping an eye on your teeth helps you to look after them well and notice any problems.

Two sets of teeth

The human body has two sets of teeth. First is the baby set of 20 teeth. These gradually fall out naturally from about the age of six. They are replaced by the adult set of 32 teeth.

Each tooth is shaped for a particular job. Your front teeth are slim and sharp to bite through food. Towards the back of your mouth, your teeth are wider and blunter, for powerful chewing.

🔍 **Give your teeth a good check every few days.**

Tooth check

Look closely at your teeth every few days. Use a bright light above, such as the light over a bathroom mirror, or a torch. Open your mouth wide and use your fingers to pull back your lips and cheeks.

Anything odd?

Look for anything unusual in your teeth. Maybe you have some new adult teeth growing, which are still quite small. Perhaps a tooth has a white patch or a wavy edge. Mention it at your next visit to the dentist. The dentist will probably say that all is well.

SCIENCE BEHIND THE MYTH

MYTH: White teeth are the strongest

SCIENCE: Not always. Slightly yellow teeth can be strong and healthy. But very yellow or very grey teeth should be checked by a dentist.

What do my teeth do?

The main jobs for teeth are to bite off lumps of food, and chew the lumps so they are soft and ready to swallow.

Biting

You can fit small food items such as peas or rice into your mouth. But not a whole melon or a complete cooked chicken! Your front teeth, called incisors, have sharp edges, like tiny spades. These slice or nibble big foods and cut off small pieces to fit into your mouth.

🔍 **Incisor teeth at the front of the mouth have sharp edges that easily cut through softer foods.**

Next to your incisors are your canine teeth. These are slightly longer and more pointed. They are good for tearing and pulling bits off foods that are difficult to bite right through.

Chewing

Your back teeth are called **premolars** and molars. Their wide, flat tops are ideal for chewing food into a soft mush for easy swallowing. As you chew food, you mix it with saliva (spit). This makes the lumps soft and slippery for swallowing. Saliva also helps to wash bits of old food off your teeth. It contains substances that protect teeth and substances that start the breakdown of food.

Practical advice

Why chewing is good

Try to chew every mouthful of food at least 30 times.

- Chewing helps to break up the food, so you get more **nutrients**.
- It prevents you choking if you try to swallow big, hard lumps.
- It helps to exercise your jaws and jaw muscles.
- It gives you time to taste delicious foods properly.

Why do baby teeth fall out?

You have only two sets of teeth during your life. There are 20 teeth in the first set, called infant, baby, or **milk teeth**. Some babies have a few teeth when they are born, but most have none. Baby teeth usually start to appear from the age of six months and are all grown by the age of three.

Once baby teeth have appeared, they cannot grow any larger. However, the jaws and the rest of the body do grow bigger. If the baby teeth stayed until adulthood, they would be too small and weak for the size of the mouth and jaws. This is why the body has a second, bigger set of teeth.

🔍 **The first baby teeth to appear are the lower incisors at the front, followed by the upper incisors above them.**

Adult teeth

When a child is about six years old, baby teeth start to fall out. The grown-up, adult, or **permanent teeth** start to appear. Usually they finish growing by the time a person is 20 years old. No more teeth will ever grow, so it is important to look after them.

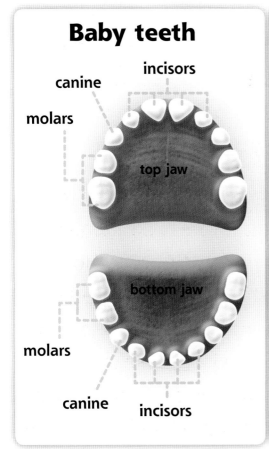

Baby teeth

incisors

canine

molars

top jaw

bottom jaw

molars

canine

incisors

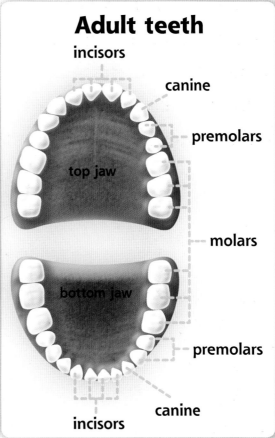

Adult teeth

incisors

canine

premolars

top jaw

molars

bottom jaw

premolars

canine

incisors

SCIENCE BEHIND THE MYTH

MYTH: Wisdom teeth make you wise.

SCIENCE: Not really. The four molar teeth at the very back of the mouth are called "wisdom teeth" because they only appear in grown-ups, who are supposed to be wise. But not all grown-ups have them. On average, about one person in five never grows wisdom teeth. Usually, this is because their mouth is too small.

What is inside a tooth?

The upper part of a tooth, which you can see above the gum, is known as the **crown**. The lower, which you cannot see, is fixed firmly into the jawbone. This part is called the **root**.

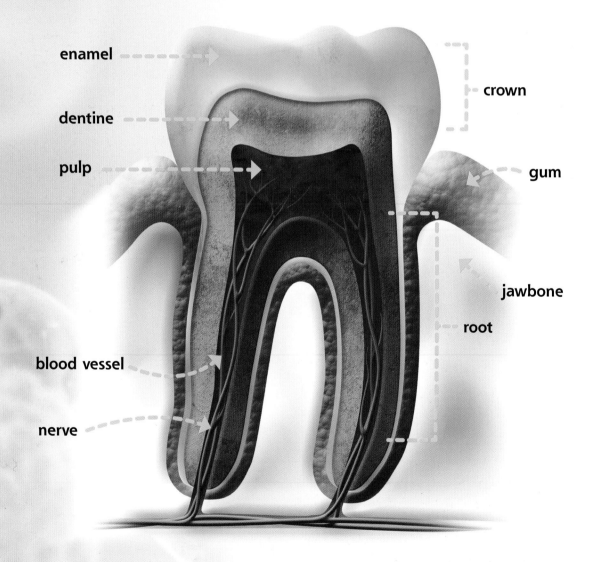

enamel

crown

dentine

pulp

gum

jawbone

root

blood vessel

nerve

This diagram shows the inside of a molar tooth.

On the outside

The outside layer of the crown is made of **enamel**. This is the hardest substance in the body, because it has to bite and chew for years without wearing away. Under the enamel is another layer, almost as hard, called **dentine**. This is more like bone and can be squashed very slightly. It helps to absorb some of the pressure as you munch and crunch hard foods.

On the inside

In the middle of a tooth is the soft **dental pulp**. This has tiny **blood vessels** that bring **nutrients** to keep the whole tooth alive and healthy. Pulp also has tiny nerves to feel problems such as too much pressure on the tooth, or toothache.

Practical advice

Broken tooth

If you break a tooth, get to the dentist quickly. If you can find the broken-off part, put it in a clean plastic bag and take it with you. The dentist will stop the tooth from becoming **infected** and start to mend it as much as possible.

What is bad for my teeth?

Many people like sweets, biscuits, cakes, chocolates, and soft drinks. But too much of these foods can be bad for the body – especially the teeth.

🔍 **Dentists often use a small mirror to help them see inside a patient's mouth.**

Sugar and acid

Sweet foods have lots of sugar in them. The problem is that sugar is also food for **bacteria**. These live on and in our bodies all the time. They usually cause no harm. However, if you eat too many sugary foods, the bacteria in your mouth feed on the sugar and produce a waste substance, acid. This acid can damage your teeth. It weakens the **enamel** and even makes holes in it. This is known as tooth decay.

Plaque

If teeth are not cleaned, old bits of food, dead bacteria, their waste, and other yucky stuff collect as a thin layer called **dental plaque**. If this is still not cleaned, it can build into thicker lumps that do great harm to the teeth and gums.

Practical advice

Protect teeth

Some high-speed sports can damage teeth. If you play them, make sure that you wear the best protection, such as a mouthguard, gumshield, or helmet.

Why do I clean my teeth?

There are many reasons to clean your teeth – to keep them and your gums healthy, to make your mouth feel fresh and clean, and to avoid the smell of bad breath.

Practical advice

When to clean teeth

The best times are after meals and at bedtime. After a meal, bacteria feed on small bits of food left in your mouth, making acid that damages tooth enamel. Cleaning your teeth at bedtime means bacteria cannot spend all night causing damage.

How to clean teeth

The three main ways to clean teeth are brushing, flossing, and using mouthwashes. Your dentist or another expert, the **dental hygienist**, can show you how. Brush every tooth on both sides, on its top, around its base with the gum, and between it and the next tooth.

Brushing also cleans food and **bacteria** off your gums. Otherwise the gums become swollen, red, and painful, and they may bleed. This type of gum disease is known as gingivitis.

Fluoride

Proper brushing needs a strong toothbrush and a toothpaste containing fluoride. The substance fluoride makes **enamel** stronger, so tooth decay is less likely. In many places, tiny amounts of fluoride are added to drinking water, to help everyone's teeth.

🔍 **The dentist or hygienist can show you how to floss without harming your teeth or gums.**

Why do I go to the dentist?

The dentist checks your teeth to make sure that you are looking after them and they are healthy, well-spaced, straight, and growing properly. The dentist also looks at the gums around the teeth to make sure they are healthy too.

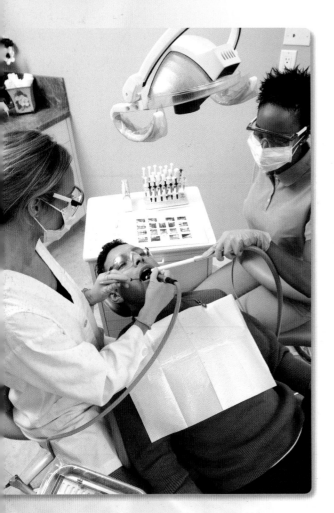

Open wide!

Most people go to the dentist every six months or each year. The dentist looks at each tooth in detail. A gurgling tube in your mouth sucks away saliva so the dentist has a clear view. He or she pokes and taps the teeth and gums to make sure they are not painful. For each visit, the dentist makes a record of the health of every tooth and of your gums.

🔍 The dentist and dental nurse use many tools and gadgets to help your teeth and gums stay healthy.

The dentist may show you how to brush and floss your teeth, and use a mouthwash. The **dental hygienist** shows you how to keep your whole mouth clean and healthy.

SCIENCE BEHIND THE MYTH

MYTH: Descaling is easy.

SCIENCE: No, it's not! Sometimes a tough substance called calculus or tartar builds up on teeth, and is like a harder version of **dental plaque**. Removing it is known as descaling, and cannot be done by ordinary tooth-brushing. The dentist has to descale teeth, usually with a tiny, powerful jet of water.

X-rays can "see" inside parts of the body. Dentists take an X-ray of the mouth so they can see any tiny cracks or holes in the teeth, the health of the gums and tooth **roots**, and any teeth still in the jawbone.

How do braces work?

Braces, also called appliances, help teeth to grow straight, look good, and stay healthy. They can also make biting and chewing more comfortable. They are fitted by the dentist or another tooth expert, the **orthodontist**.

Made to measure

Most types of braces press on the teeth gently and for a long time. This slowly pushes the teeth as they grow, to make them straighter and fit together properly. Each brace is made to measure, to fit just one person. The dentist or orthodontist must check and adjust it regularly.

🔍 **This child is having braces fitted on to her teeth.**

SCIENCE BEHIND THE MYTH

MYTH: Braces always hurt.

SCIENCE: If braces are fitted properly, and the wearer gets used to them, they should not hurt. If they do, they may have been pushed out of shape. The wearer should go back to the dentist.

Types of braces

Fixed braces stay in the mouth for long periods, perhaps months. Removable braces can be taken out by the wearer for cleaning or on special occasions. Head braces have a frame that fits around the head and are usually worn at night.

Sometimes teeth are too crowded. The dentist may take out one or two and use a brace to move the other teeth along to fill the gap.

Practical advice

Caring for teeth when wearing a brace

When wearing braces, tooth cleaning is even more important. Cutting down on sticky or sugary foods and drinks is vital. The dentist may also advise a special fluoride cream or a germ-killing mouthwash.

What is toothache?

If people do not keep their teeth and gums healthy, sooner or later they will get toothache. This is one of the worst pains. It can hurt terribly until the dentist treats it.

Eating away teeth

As **bacteria** feed on old food in the mouth, they produce acids that eat into the tooth **enamel**, making it soft and weak. This is tooth decay. If the tooth is not mended, eventually a hole or cavity appears. Fluid from the mouth leaks into the tooth's **dental pulp** and affects the nerves there, causing toothache.

Practical advice

Help for toothache

If you have a toothache but cannot see the dentist straight away, there are several things you can do:

- Use a dental mouthwash or a mouth rinse of warm, slightly salty water.
- Use a special cream from the chemist on your gums to ease the pain.
- Avoid hard, crunchy foods.

Tooth abscess

Sometimes germs get into the pulp inside the tooth, making it start to swell and hurt. This **infection** can spread down the **root** into the jawbone, producing a horrible-tasting liquid called pus. This may form a painful swelling known as an abscess.

SCIENCE BEHIND THE MYTH

MYTH: Toothache can get better on its own.

SCIENCE: This is not true. A sprained wrist or a cut finger usually gets better. But left alone, toothache nearly always gets worse. The only cure is a trip to the dentist.

tooth decay (cavity caused by bacteria)

enamel

dentine

pulp

crown

gum

jawbone

root

blood vessel
nerve

If not treated, tooth decay can eat away enamel and **dentine** and get into the soft, sensitive pulp.

How are teeth mended?

If tooth decay is just beginning, the dentist may be able to treat it by painting a special liquid on to the tooth. If the decay is deeper, the usual way to mend it is to put in a filling.

Drill and fill

To repair a decayed tooth, the dentist first gives the patient an injection to prevent pain. Then the decayed part of the tooth is quickly drilled away to make a clean hole. Into this is put a very hard substance, the filling. Some fillings are made from several substances, mixed to be the same colour as the tooth. Other fillings are made of metal, and are a silvery colour. Another choice is a gold metal filling.

🔍 **Metal fillings are usually a silvery substance called amalgam.**

Taken out

If the decay is quite bad, the dentist may remove most of the tooth's upper part and put on a false top, called a dental **crown**. With really bad decay, the whole tooth may have to be taken out. A false tooth, made of very hard plastic or metal, can be put in its place.

SCIENCE BEHIND THE MYTH

MYTH: False teeth soon wear away.

SCIENCE: Some people think that false teeth, called **dentures**, are weak and soon wear away. But modern false teeth are extremely strong and tough. A whole false tooth, including the **root**, is called a tooth implant. Modern tooth implants made from the metal titanium are almost as hard as a real tooth.

How can I take care of my teeth?

If your teeth are not healthy, they soon let you know. You might get toothache and have trouble eating and talking. You only have one set of grown-up teeth, so look after them well!

Happy teeth checklist

Remember the main ways to look after your teeth:

- Do not eat too many sweet or sugary foods.
- Avoid snacks and sweets between meals.
- Clean teeth at least twice a day – after breakfast and before bed. If possible, clean them after every meal.
- Brush your teeth with a fluoride toothpaste, and use floss and mouthwash if the dentist says these are right for you.
- Visit the dentist once or twice each year for a full check-up.
- If you get toothache, or break a tooth in an accident, see the dentist as soon as possible.
- Keep smiling!

SCIENCE BEHIND THE MYTH

MYTH: Some foods clean your teeth.

SCIENCE: This is not true. Some people say that if you eat certain foods, such as apples, you do not have to clean your teeth afterwards. But any food can leave bits in the mouth for the **bacteria** to eat. However, eating does make saliva come into the mouth, which helps to protect teeth. A dry mouth is bad for teeth.

Thorough cleaning and help from braces will make teeth look good and last a lifetime.

The body's two sets of teeth

Everyone's teeth are different in size, shape, and colour. They grow and fall out at different times. But most people have teeth like those shown here. Look in the mirror and compare your own teeth to the pictures on this page.

Baby teeth and when they appear

incisor 1 (8–12 months)

canine (16–22 months)

incisor 2 (9–13 months)

Molars are known as "cheek teeth" because they are on the insides of the cheeks.

upper jaw

molar 1 (13–19 months)

molar 2 (25–33 months)

molar 2 (23–31 months)

molar 1 (14–18 months)

lower jaw

canine (17–23 months)

incisor 2 (10–16 months)

incisor 1 (6–10 months)

Canines are good to rip and tear food.

Total: 20 teeth

Incisors are best for biting, slicing, and nibbling.

Premolars chew and squash foods.

Adult teeth and when they appear

canine (11–12 years)

incisor 1 (7–8 years)

incisor 2 (8–9 years)

The canine is sometimes called the "eye tooth" because it is directly below the eye.

upper jaw

premolar 1 (10–11 years)

premolar 2 (10–12 years)

molar 1 (6–7 years)

molar 2 (12–13 years)

molar 3 (17–21 years)

lower jaw

molar 3 (17–21 years)

molar 2 (11–13 years)

molar 1 (6–7 years)

premolar 2 (11–12 years)

premolar 1 (10–11 years)

canine (9–10 years)

incisor 2 (7–8 years)

incisor 1 (6–7 years)

The four molar 3 teeth, at the back of each side of the jaw, are the "wisdom teeth". You may only grow these if your mouth is big enough. In some people, they never appear, but they might be under the gums.

Total: 32 teeth

Molars are most powerful for crushing and crunching.

Glossary

bacteria tiny living things, too small to see except under a microscope. Some types cause infection and disease.

blood vessel pipe-like tube that carries blood around the body

crown upper part of a tooth which is covered with enamel and shows above the gum

dental hygienist expert in keeping teeth, gums, and the whole mouth clean and healthy

dental plaque gooey mixture of old food, living and dead bacteria, and acid, which can build up on teeth

dental pulp soft inner part of a tooth, with nerves and blood vessels

dentine hard middle layer of a tooth, between the enamel and the pulp

dentures false teeth on a removable plate that fits on to the gums

enamel extremely hard outer layer of a tooth

infection when germs get into a body part and cause disease

milk teeth baby teeth; the body's first set of teeth

nutrient substance needed by the body for energy and to grow and repair itself

orthodontist specialist in treating crooked, crowded, or gappy teeth, and other similar problems

permanent teeth adult teeth; the body's second and last set of teeth

premolars fairly wide, flat-topped teeth towards the rear of the mouth, between the canines and the molars

root in a tooth, the lower part of the tooth that fixes it in the jawbone below the gum

Find out more

Books

Dentist (People Who Help Us), Rebecca Hunter
(Cherrytree Books, 2006)

Taking Care of Your Teeth (Healthy Kids), Sylvia Goulding
(Cherrytree Books, 2006)

Websites

kidshealth.org/kid/htbw/teeth.html

You can read several information-packed articles about teeth on this website.

www.childrenfirst.nhs.uk/kids/health/ask_doc/c/ clean_teeth.html

Visit this website to find out why we should clean our teeth, all about the life of a tooth, and for advice about fillings.

www.mouthpower.org/mouthpower.cfm

This fun website has lots of toothy games and activities.

Index